LOOKING UP IN

EDINBURGH AS YOU HAVE NEVER SEEN IT BEFORE

JANE PEYTON

Photographs by Helen Peyton
Series designed by Liz Sephton

⊛ WILEY-ACADEMY

In memory of our Mum, Angela, whom we looked up to.

Published in Great Britain in 2004 by Wiley-Academy, a division of John Wiley & Sons Ltd

Copyright © 2004   John Wiley & Sons Ltd, The Atrium, Southern Gate, Chichester, West Sussex PO19 8SQ, England
Telephone   (+44) 1243 779777

Email (for orders and customer service enquiries): cs-books@wiley.co.uk
Visit our Home Page on www.wileyeurope.com or www.wiley.com

Other Wiley Editorial Offices
John Wiley & Sons Inc., 111 River Street, Hoboken, NJ 07030, USA
Jossey-Bass, 989 Market Street, San Francisco, CA 94103-1741, USA
Wiley-VCH Verlag GmbH, Boschstr. 12, D-69469 Weinheim, Germany
John Wiley & Sons Australia Ltd, 33 Park Road, Milton, Queensland 4064, Australia
John Wiley & Sons (Asia) Pte Ltd, 2 Clementi Loop #02-01, Jin Xing Distripark, Singapore 129809
John Wiley & Sons Canada Ltd, 22 Worcester Road, Etobicoke, Ontario, Canada M9W 1L1

ISBN 0-470-09147-9

Cover design, origination and layout: Artmedia Press Ltd, London
Maps: Louisa Fitch

Printed and bound in Italy by Conti Tipocolor

CONTENTS

PREFACE

My first memory of Edinburgh is a visit when I was seven years old. I pointed to a modest turreted tower near Calton Hill and said to my parents incredulously, 'Is that the castle – it's a bit small isn't it?' A few minutes later, the spectacle of Edinburgh Castle towering on its rock came into view and I have never forgotten it.

Looking Up in Edinburgh is divided into three sections – Fountainbridge and Old Town, Royal Mile and New Town. I did explore other parts of the city but decided on a limited geographical area so readers could leisurely visit all the sites on foot in one day.

Many people helped me with this project and I am deeply grateful to them. Thank you to Tony Harman of Maple Leaf Images, Skipton, North Yorkshire who has turned out to be the unofficial sponsor of the *Looking Up* series. Just as he did for the previous book, *Looking Up in London,* Tony kindly lent us his camera equipment and hand-developed the photographs so they looked their best. Abigail Grater was so generous with the key to her Edinburgh flat and even pointed out where the chocolate biscuits were stashed, then left me to them. Nicole Cantu, many thanks for your generosity and financial advice. Louisa Fitch, thanks for designing the lovely maps and book website. Thanks also to George Naylor for his technical expertise with the website. Thank you to Liz Sephton, who designed the gorgeous colour scheme and layout of the book. Thanks very much also to Helen Castle, Oriana Di Mascio, Colin Howarth, Mariangela Palazzi-Williams, Famida Rasheed, Felicity Roberts and Scott Smith. And to computer expert Ali Ulugun who was so helpful and managed to retrieve all my files from a terminally damaged laptop – a special thank you.

Thank you to all the archivists, marketing and publicity executives, property managers and historians who supplied information about buildings featured in the book. The Edinburgh Room of the Central Library was an invaluable resource and I spent several days looking through its archives. It was very handy for the Monster Mash café on Forrest Road with its peerless comfort food.

To St Jude and St Anthony – a big thanks for sending sun and blue skies the majority of times we asked, despite it being winter when the photographs were shot.

Finally, thanks to Maggie Toy: had she not commissioned *Looking Up in London*, this book would not exist.

Jane Peyton

REVIEWS FOR LOOKING UP IN LONDON

"Jane Peyton has put together a delightful guide to the details we so seldom see because we rarely raise our eyes above the pavement…"
The Bookseller: Art, Architecture and Photography Supplement

"Full of fascinating facts and intriguing images, it's sure to appeal to all explorers of the city, leaving the rest scurrying along the streets looking straight ahead"
What's on in London

"If you catch its infectious zeal for all things upwards you may find yourself walking into lampposts…[Miss Peyton] has the energy of an enthusiast…"
Belgravia

"…aims to tell the story of London's urban development in a simple, light-hearted fashion"
New Urban Futures

"This interesting book will no doubt start a new hobby for many readers…I found the book very entertaining and can recommend it to anyone interested in architecture or the history of London"
Building Design

"A compendium of stunning photographs and fascinating facts, it will appeal to all explorers of the city who appreciate their surroundings – visitors and residents alike"
This is London

PLAYING THE LOOKING UP IN EDINBURGH GAME

Your mission, if you choose to accept it, is to explore Edinburgh, searching for the architectural treasures featured in this book. Imagine yourself as a detective and put your best sleuthing foot forward. You are on a journey to discover the incredible buildings that combine to make Edinburgh such an unforgettable city.

This book is the key to a secret Edinburgh. It will enable you to see the city in a manner that people who hurry along the streets looking straight ahead do not. Entering Edinburgh's hidden world is simple, just look up above eye-level and prepare for a surprise. Goddesses, dragons and cherubs are gazing down, waiting to be admired.

Beginning in the Lothian Road area of Edinburgh, you are directed with the help of a simple map through three central districts of the city. Along the route are the remarkable architectural and decorative jewels featured in the photographs. The goal is to find them, using the book as a guide. (In several instances, there are two separate photographs of the same location.)

Three clues about each mystery site are provided.
1. The name of the street on which it is located.
2. A map grid reference.
3. A cryptic clue about the location or its vicinity (the answer is in the building's address).

Arm yourself with a detailed map of Edinburgh's Old and New Town and slip on some comfortable footwear. Once on the route, start looking up until you identify the locations in the photographs. To learn more about each site, turn the page for some brief historical facts.

If sleuthing is not your style, you can still explore Edinburgh above eye-level using the book as a straightforward travel guide. The exact street address is listed overleaf of the photograph.

To be honest, your mission will never be complete. Once you start looking up, you will be unable to stop, no matter where you are.

INTRODUCTION
EDINBURGH – A DREAM IN MASONRY

…this profusion of eccentricities, this dream in masonry and living rock, is not a dropscene in a theatre but a city in the world of everyday reality…

Breathtaking. Monumental. Dramatic. From all directions, Edinburgh presents a stunning visual overture. With its towering castle on a crag hundreds of feet high, flanked by impossibly tall tenements that hug a mile long ridge, then down below, imposing Graeco-Roman public buildings, Edinburgh could be the make-believe of a set designer. How can this schizophrenic combination of medieval Old Town and classical New Town be real? It is quite a story...

No situation could be more commanding for the head city of a kingdom; none better chosen for noble prospects. From her tall precipice and terraced gardens she looks far and wide on the sea and broad champaigns.

Blame it on the men in armour. Without the risk of attack from hostile armed forces, Edinburgh would not be situated where it is nor look the way it does.

It was a Celtic tribe known as the Votadini (aka Gododdin) that recognised the defensive attributes of the Castle rock and founded a tiny settlement they called Din Eidyn (meaning 'fortress of the hill slope'). With the invasion of Angle warriors in 638, Din Eidyn was annexed for the Kingdom of Northumbria. Whilst the Castle rock appeared to be impregnable from the north, south and west, an approach from the east up the ridge of what is now Royal Mile was straightforward. Throughout the Castle's history invaders captured it time and time again.

Scotland as a nation did not exist until the 11th century. Until then, tribes and clans inhabited land the Romans called Caledonia. Bloodshed was common as Vikings, Angles, Saxons, Scots and Picts battled for power. A first step towards nationhood was taken in 843 when clan leader Kenneth MacAlpin united the Scots and Picts north of the Firth of Forth. Angles in the south resisted the newly dominant Scots but by 1018, they were defeated and Scottish rule extended over what is now Scotland. Peace was elusive however, because the emergence of a cohesive nation led to conflict with England and enmity between the two countries lasted for the next six centuries.

Din Eidyn, with its wooden fort and flimsy settlement of huts, was insignificant to the Scots. But when King Malcolm Canmore built a hunting lodge on top of the Castle rock in the late 11th century, Din Eidyn's importance increased. It was Malcolm's son, King David I who fortified and expanded the lodge to become his primary residence and moved the Royal Court from the capital in Dunfermline to Edinburgh Castle. David's mark upon history is not just confined to the Castle, for he also founded Holyrood Abbey and his motive for doing so added to the saga of Edinburgh. On the feast day of the Holy Cross (rood) whilst David was stag hunting, he fell from his horse. The stag turned to attack and as the king prayed for his life, he saw a cross of fire appear between the beast's horns. Suddenly it turned and ran away. In gratitude for his salvation, David ordered the construction of an abbey to be named in honour of the Holy Rood and built on the site of his miraculous escape.

Edinburgh was only 80 kilometres from the border with England and as relations were often unfriendly there was a real danger of attack by English troops. A town wall was erected and a stream was diverted to create a defensive stretch of water known as Nor' Loch to the north of Castle rock. Although the walls seldom held back invaders, the citizens of Edinburgh chose to live within them for security. Perched on a rocky crag with steep slopes and limited flat land, the only direction for Edinburgh to expand was upwards. Given the geographical constraints faced by architects and builders, they were ingenious in creating a unique townscape. People lived in Europe's first multi-storey apartment blocks or tenements (also known as lands). Tenements were accessed along narrow wynds – alleyways open at both ends, or by closes, many of which had originally been fruit and vegetable market gardens (enclosures). As the population increased, the gardens were sacrificed to build more housing. The word enclosure was shortened to 'close' and the former gardens became courtyards for entry to the lands.

This old black city, which was all the world like a rabbit-warren, not only by the number of its indwellers, but the complication of its passages and holes.

Edinburgh began to flourish and during the

reign of King James II (1437–60) it became Scotland's capital. Trade through the nearby port of Leith increased, with commodities such as skins, grain, herring, coal, wool and linen exported to the Continent. Traders grew rich and their prosperity allowed them to build expensive stone houses in what was still a medieval wooden town.

It was King James IV who decided that a palace would be cosier than a draughty old castle so he moved into the newly built Holyroodhouse in 1504. During his reign the road between Holyrood and the Castle became known as the Royal Mile and the buildings of both Edinburgh and Canongate, the ecclesiastical quarter and independent burgh that served the Abbey, extended along this road towards each other.

Only sixty or so closes and wynds now remain of the hundreds that previously existed. Down these alleyways, overcrowded tenements housed thousands of people, often in unsavoury conditions. Edinburgh was filthy, with no sanitary plumbing or sewers and inadequate water supplies. Outbreaks of cholera and typhus were common. Pigs and dogs roamed the streets competing with rats for scraps. A contemporary quote describes the wynds as '*mud overlaid and coverit with middingis and with the filthe and excrementis of man and beast*'. Each night at 10pm drum beats echoed through the town and a chorus of 'Gardyloo' (*gardez l'eau* — watch out for the water) could be heard as slops and sewage or 'night soil' were thrown out of the windows to the streets below. (The term gardyloo is believed to be the source of loo, the slang word for toilet.) Pedestrians could hire guides to lead them through the night and shout 'haud yer haunde' (hold your hand), beseeching householders above to stop pouring the slops momentarily. Despite such foul living conditions and overcrowding, Edinburgh was a magnet and it continued to grow.

> *Far set in fields and woods, the town I see,*
> *Spring gallant from the shallows of her smoke,*
> *Cragged, spired and turreted.*

Edinburgh's population reached approximately 40,000 by the early 17th century. New housing was urgently required so extra storeys were built on top of existing tenements. An example of this resourceful solution to the housing crisis can be seen at John Knox House, High Street – originally it was a two-storey townhouse. Stinky, polluted Edinburgh earned the nickname, Auld Reekie (Old Smoky) for the pall of smoke hanging over it, caused by thousands of wood and coal-burning stoves. Outbreaks of fire were common and flames spread quickly in the cramped wynds and closes. Damage to buildings was exacerbated by shoddy construction and the use of flammable wood and thatch, so from 1620, strict building codes stipulated stone facades and stone or slate roofs. The blueprint of the Old Town seen today was ordained.

Edinburgh was a convivial place – it had to be with people of all social standing and incomes living in such limited space. Brilliant intellectuals rubbed shoulders with the illiterate, wealthy lawyers shared the pavement with paupers. Vibrant, noisy and crowded, solitude was impossible. An English visitor described it as a place of *'odious smells, barbarous sounds, bad suppers, excellent hearts and most enlightened and cultivated understandings'.*

With the death of Queen Elizabeth in 1603, Scotland's King James VI acceded to the English throne and united the two kingdoms. For the first time, Edinburgh's citizens lived without fear of invasion as James ruled over the longest period of reconciliation the two nations had known. It was a brief respite – after James' death Scottish and English blood was spilled as the two nations skirmished for the next 80 years.

Lasting peace came at a great price for Scotland. In 1707, the Act of Union was signed, uniting the Parliaments of England and Scotland, with England as the dominant partner and the nation's capital in London. Scotland, no longer independent, became a constituent of the United Kingdom. Edinburgh was diminished, relegated to provincial city status and dubbed the 'Widow's Metropolis'. But she was not down for long and recovered in spectacular fashion – thanks to the genius of her intelligentsia and the imagination of her architects.

> *…an earthly city, illustrious for her beauty, her tragic and picturesque associations, and for the credit of some of her brave sons.*

Edinburgh's peace dividend coincided with the flowering of Scottish Enlightenment in the mid-18th century. The Enlightenment was a period of new thinking in areas such as philosophy, economics, law, medicine and architecture. Edinburgh was home to scholars such as philosopher David Hume, geologist James Hutton, economist Adam Smith and architect Robert Adam. Edinburgh may not have been Britain's primary city but it could claim to be an intellectual capital and soon it was to become one of the singular cities of the world – and all because of town planning.

By the turn of the 18th century, 50,000 souls were crammed into Auld Reekie and it was ready to burst. The Act of Union meant that residents of Edinburgh no longer had to fear the old enemy so the defensive wall that had restricted the town's horizontal growth was demolished. When a Royal Mile tenement collapsed in 1751, the run-down nature of Edinburgh became apparent. Construction of North Bridge improved access to Leith and highlighted acres of rural land ripe for development. Out of the fields beyond Nor' Loch arose elegant streets, squares, crescents and gardens. This new Edinburgh would be no imperial city as London was; instead, homage was paid to ancient Athens, birthplace of democracy and great philosophers and home of classical architecture.

Merchants, nobles, lawyers, and anyone else who could afford to, abandoned medieval Edinburgh. In doing so a hitherto unknown social apartheid grew up between the wealthy in New Town and the poor left behind in Old Town. Edinburgh was now a city of 'us and them', with those in the new community living in great comfort and the residents of the ancient town trapped in a decaying infrastructure.

Few places if any offer a more barbaric display of contrasts to the eye. In the very midst stands one of the most satisfactory crags in nature – a Bass Rock upon dry land, rooted in a garden shaken by passing trains, carrying a crown of battlements and turrets, and describing its warlike shadow over the liveliest and brightest thoroughfare of the New Town.

Nowhere outside Greece displayed such extensive classical architecture as Edinburgh did. With public buildings and monuments that resembled Ancient Greek temples in Princes Gardens and on Calton Hill, Edinburgh earned the moniker '*Athens of the North*'. Edinburgh's residents had reason to be proud of their magnificent city — as long as they admired the view with their backs to Old Town.

By 1827, when the Improvement Act was passed, Old Town had deteriorated into slum conditions. Refurbishment commenced, inspired by local hero Walter Scott. His novels celebrated Scotland's heritage and traditions, and had brought about a new pride and appreciation of all things Scottish. Known as the 'tartanisation' of Scotland it included a face-lift for parts of Old Town that reappeared to show off a Scottish Baronial style of turrets and battlements. A number of lands were demolished and new thoroughfares such as Cockburn Street took their place. An educational quarter with grand university buildings was established to the south of Royal Mile between North and South Bridge. However, attempts to rescue Old Town were not enough and so its decline continued. Other tenements collapsed and Canongate and Grassmarket in particular slid further into disrepair. Meanwhile, Edinburgh was expanding in all directions – new tenements were built in Marchmont and Bruntfield, and luxury villas with gardens appeared in Morningside and Colinton. Victorian optimism and philanthropy spurred the construction of public schools, hospitals, churches, galleries and banks but this dynamism contrasted with poor medieval Old Town. From its brooding eyrie on Castle rock, Old Town seemed to glare down on its bright, clean, well-maintained and above all modern, younger sisters.

Yet Old Town had a champion. Patrick Geddes, considered to be a founder of modern urban planning, recognised the significance of Old Town in the story of Edinburgh. During the 1880s several tenements on Lawnmarket were renovated under his plan for the area's renaissance; he backed the construction of the brown and white confection – known as Ramsay Gardens – next to the Castle. This building enticed intellectuals to reside in Old Town, no longer was it just the poor who lived in Edinburgh's historic heart. Restoration was by now in vogue and the Cockburn Association became one of the world's first preservation societies, with a mission to conserve the city's architectural legacy.

Edinburgh suffered little bomb damage from air raids during World War II. In the immediate post-war period, a city improvement plan authorised the clearance of slum tenements in Old Town. Residents were relocated to new suburban housing estates. The human soul of the ancient town was disappearing.

New Town sustained a visual wound during the 1960s when many of Princes Street's Victorian buildings were demolished and replaced by unimaginative structures that offered no respect to the street's spectacular prospect. Brutalism made its mark with a concrete eyesore called St James' Centre, often voted the least popular building in Scotland. When Edinburgh's citizens saw how their city was being altered architecturally, the council was widely criticised. Strict planning guidelines were introduced, for instance, any new building on the Royal Mile was required to resemble a medieval tenement and harmonise with its neighbours. Conservation groups were established and with them came an increased appreciation of Edinburgh's unique heritage.

It is the beautiful that I thus actively recall, the august airs of the castle on its rock, nocturnal passages of lights and trees…

In 1995, the United Nations Education, Scientific and Cultural Organisation (UNESCO) honoured Edinburgh when the status of World Heritage Site was bestowed for the city's exceptional historical and cultural interest. However, Edinburgh is not a historical theme park frozen in time. Modern buildings, such as the Festival Theatre, Museum of Scotland extension and Scottish Parliament building on Canongate prove that architecturally the city looks forward too.

Unforgettable and peerless, Edinburgh has bewitched visitors and residents alike for centuries. As Queen Victoria wrote in her diary, describing a visit to a city she loved,

> *The view of Edinburgh from the road before you enter Leith is quite enchanting. It is, as Albert said, fairy-like.*

Note: The quotations are by Robert Louis Stevenson from letters and essays he wrote about his hometown, Edinburgh.

Fountainbridge/Old Town

a   b   c   d   e

1

THE CASTLE

MOUND PLACE
BANK STREET
RAMSAY LANE
CAMBRIDGE STREET
CASTLE TERRACE
CASTLEHILL LAWNMARKET
HIGH STREET
JOHNSTON TERRACE
LOTHIAN ROAD
GRINDLEY ST.
SPITTAL ST.
KINGS STABLE ROAD
WEST BOW
GEORGE IV BRIDGE
GRASS MARKET
COWGATE
2
BREAD STREET
WEST PORT
CANDLEMAKER ROW
FOUNTAINBRIDGE
GREYFRIARS
KIRK
LADY LAURISTON ST.
LAURISTON STREET
EARL GREY ST.
FORREST ROAD
BRISTO PLACE
3
LAURISTON PLACE
LAURISTON PLACE
TEVIOT PLACE
BRISTO
SQUARE

■ walking route

■ major streets

■ location of photograph

■ park, square or open space

Fountainbridge / Old Town

Location	Lothian Road, EH3, east side of the street
Map grid	1A
Architect	J Stockdale Harrison. Lion keystones by Hubert Paton
Built	1910–14
Style	Beaux-Arts
Cryptic clue	Who directs you to your theatre seat?

Address

Usher Hall, Lothian Road, EH3

'I have so much money that I do not know what to do with it'. With that statement by brewing magnate Andrew Usher, the idea for a grand concert venue in Edinburgh was born. Usher donated £100,000 to build the hall that bears his name. The Deed of the Gift stated that the hall should be used primarily for music, although other purposes could be accommodated. 'Other purposes' were often political. Prime Minister Herbert Asquith spoke at Usher Hall in 1914 to justify World War I and recruit soldiers. In 1934, the hall was host to an assembly of the British Union of Fascists, addressed by Oswald Mosley. It caused a riot as 6,000 anti-fascists gathered outside, jostled delegates and stoned buses on Lothian Road. With the outbreak of Spain's civil war in 1936, ideologues from both sides of the conflict held rallies at Usher Hall with the aim of signing up volunteers

to fight for General Franco's fascists or the opposition International Brigades. A memorial plaque to Scottish veterans who fought in this war to defeat fascism stands in Princes Street Gardens.

The crouching figures that embellish Usher Hall's facade represent Music of the Woods and Sea, Soul of the Sea and Municipal Beneficence.

Location	Lothian Road, EH3, east side of the street
Map grid	2A
Architect	Not known
Built	19th century
Style	Classical
Cryptic clue	Music Hall Marie and Tango Sierra Bravo

Address

Lloyds TSB, 165 Lothian Road, EH3

Customers entering Lloyds TSB Fountainbridge branch walk under a mosaic bearing words spoken by Shylock the moneylender in Shakespeare's play, *The Merchant of Venice.*

This was a way to thrive, and he was blest:
And thrift is blessing, if men steal it not.

According to local lore, Lothian Road was built in one day by a gang of labourers, funded by a wealthy Edinburgh man for a bet. There is no proof to the veracity of this tale but, as the council did not pay for the road, who did and why?

Location	Intersection of Bread Street and East Fountainbridge, EH3
Map grid	2B
Architect	T P Marwick
Built	1914
Style	Baroque
Cryptic clue	Score in a game or the sharp end of a stick

Address

Edinburgh's Point Hotel inhabits the premises of a former co-operative department store named after St Cuthbert, the hermit monk of Lindisfarne.

Bread Street most likely takes its name from the Bread Society that was based there in the 19th century. Fountainbridge was the name of a suburb, first recorded in 1713. The fountain (well) by a bridge over the local stream was considered '*singularly sweet water*'. Originally the area's name was Foulbrigs and appeared on maps in 1512. Foul, pronounced in Scots as *fool,* means muddy – *brigs* could refer to a bridge or to the brighouse (tollhouse) that operated nearby.

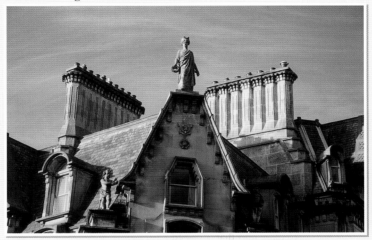

Location	Castle Terrace, EH1, north west side of the street
Map grid	2B
Architect	James Gowans
Built	1868
Style	A mix of Continental styles and Arts & Crafts
Cryptic clue	Where would-be Nightingales train, regally

Address

Queen Victoria gazes imperiously from the roof of 31 Castle Terrace but she is overshadowed by the sheer drama of the citadel towering above on a seemingly unassailable rock. Much of the Castle's structure dates from the 17th and 18th centuries, although within its walls is Edinburgh's oldest building, an 11th century chapel dedicated to (Queen) St Margaret, wife of King Malcolm Canmore.

As part of a scheme to raise funds for the Royal Purse in the 1620s, King Charles I decreed that a patch of ground in the Castle was Nova Scotian territory. In exchange for 1,000 marks, donors were granted the title Baronet of Nova Scotia (Latin for New Scotland) and thousands of acres of land in the new colony. As a token, the baronets were given a piece of turf from the Castle's Nova Scotian corner. A plaque near the Castle gates commemorates this anomaly. New Scotland in Old Scotland is now buried underneath the Esplanade.

Location	West Port, EH1, south side of the street
Map grid	2B
Architect	David McArthy
Built	1887
Style	Scottish tenement
Cryptic clue	Where shoemakers hail from

Address

Cordiners Land, 64 West Port, EH1

West Port was a gate in the town wall and also the name of the route down to Grassmarket. For over 400 years until the beginning of the 20th century, livestock herded from the west took a final walk along West Port to Grassmarket where they were slaughtered and butchered. Death was not just confined to animals though, because humans were executed there until 1784 when the last public hanging took place. The gibbet was outside a pub called The Last Drop, named to commemorate the final execution.

West Port was the home of two of Edinburgh's most notorious residents –William Burke and William Hare. In 1827 when one of their lodgers died before paying his rent, Burke and Hare saw an opportunity to recoup the lost money and sold the body to Dr Knox at Edinburgh University School of Anatomy. At that time, the School had difficulty obtaining bodies for use in dissection class so no questions were asked when cadavers were made available. Burke and Hare built up a lucrative trade selling fresh corpses to the School but in doing so they had resorted to murder.

Up to 30 people are thought to have died at the hands of Burke and Hare – all strangled or suffocated so the exterior of the precious commodity was not damaged. After they were captured, Hare turned King's evidence and escaped execution unlike Burke, whose corpse, ironically was donated to the School of Anatomy and dissected.

Location	Grassmarket, EH1, north side of the street
Map grid	2C
Architect	Not known
Built	Early 18th century
Style	Classical
Cryptic clue	Alternative word for stag, not black

Address

White Hart Inn, 34 Grassmarket, EH1

Established in 1516, the White Hart is the oldest surviving public house in Edinburgh. Whilst the cellar dates from the 16th century, the building above ground is 18th century. Its name relates to an event in 1128 when King David I was hunting on the feast day of the Holy Rood (cross) and fell from his horse as he chased a stag (hart). The angry beast turned on the king and as David prayed for his life, he saw a fiery cross appear between the animal's antlers. Suddenly the stag ran away. In gratitude for his escape, the King founded Holyrood Abbey.

Poet Robert Burns is thought to have written his love song *Ae Fond Kiss* whilst staying at the White Hart in 1791. Burke and Hare lured drunken patrons from the inn back to their residence, murdered them and sold the corpses to Edinburgh School of Anatomy. Although they are always referred to as body snatchers, there is no evidence that Burke and Hare ever stole bodies from graves and at his trial Burke denied it.

Visible damage on the White Hart sign was caused when a bomb, dropped from a German Zeppelin during World War I, landed on the pavement outside. The explosion blew out windows on Grassmarket and West Bow but there were no serious injuries.

Location	Greyfriars Kirk, west side of the graveyard
Map grid	2D
Architect	Not known
Built	Not known
Style	Classical
Cryptic clue	The dear departed

Address

Greyfriars Kirk, 1 Greyfriars Place, EH1

Greyfriars Kirk graveyard was one of Edinburgh's most prestigious final resting places and an estimated 80,000 corpses are buried there. Poet Christopher North described it as, '*A sublime cemetery, yet I sud'na like to be interr'd in't. It looks see dank and clammy and cauld*'.

In the southwest corner stands the Martyrs Monument, a memorial to the National Covenanters. These were Scottish Presbyterians had signed the National Covenant at Greyfriars Kirk, some in their own blood, against the imposition by King Charles I of the Book of Common Prayer. In 1639, 1,200 signatories were imprisoned for several months in a fenced off section of the churchyard. Some died of exposure or starvation, others were freed, but recalcitrant Covenanters were either transported as slaves to the West Indies or executed by hanging in Grassmarket. Ironically, the body of 'Bloody' George Mackenzie, who harshly prosecuted the Covenanters, is interred in a family tomb not far from the

Martyrs Monument. His restless spirit is said to haunt the graveyard. Schoolboys used to dance around his mausoleum and shout: '*Bluidy MacKenzie, come out if ye daur, Lift the sneck and draw the bar.*'

The gravestone in the photograph is one of several elaborate memorials that stand against the west wall in Greyfriars churchyard. Notable Scots buried here include architect James Craig who planned the first New Town and poet Allan Ramsay who established Britain's first library of circulating books.

Location	Forrest Road, EH1, east side of the street
Map grid	3E
Architect	J C Hay
Built	19th century
Style	Scottish Baronial
Cryptic clue	Unusual comrades and associates meet here

Address

Oddfellows Hall, 12–14 Forrest Road, EH1

Oddfellow is a term that dates back to medieval trade guilds. Fellows were freelancers or journeymen (from the Latin word for day) who were paid by the day for their work. Guilds were fraternities that offered members support and protection. In towns and villages where there were insufficient Fellows of a particular trade to form an exclusive guild, men from an odd assortment of trades formed groups, and these came to be known as Oddfellows.

Today's Oddfellows is a non-profit friendly society that exists to support members in times of need. The concept of mutual support can be traced to the Roman era when groups of legionnaires would make regular financial deposits, literally into a pot. In the case of injury or retirement from service, money from the pot was available to contributors.

Faith, Hope and Charity are represented in the panel above the hall's entrance.

Location   Bristo Square, EH1, west side of the square
Map grid   3E
Built   1887
Cryptic clue   Combine part of his surname and forename to switch on this
                light sabre at (Jedi) night

Address

McEwan Lamp, Bristo Square, EH1

Known as the McEwan Lamp, this ornate streetlight was presented to the city of Edinburgh by its Member of Parliament, William McEwan. Electricity had been installed in the city two years previously. Before then, streetlighting was gas fired. As darkness fell, a 'leerie' or lamplighter visited each lamp and climbed a ladder to light it.

Robert Louis Stevenson describes it in his children's poem, *The Lamplighter*:

My tea is nearly ready and the sun has left the sky,
It's time to take the window to see Leerie going by.
For every night at teatime and before you take your seat,
With lantern and with ladder he comes posting up the street.
Now Tom would be a driver and Maria go to sea,
And my papa's a banker and as rich as he can be,
But I, when I am stronger and can choose what I'm to do,
O Leerie, I'll go round at night and light the lamps with you!
For we are very lucky, with a lamp before the door,
And Leerie stops to light it as he lights so many more.
And O! before you hurry by with ladder and with light,
O Leerie, see a little child and nod to him tonight!

Location	Teviot Place, EH1, south side of the street
Map grid	3E
Architect	Robert Rowand Anderson
Built	1888–97
Style	Italian Renaissance
Cryptic clue	Graduate to Export Ale

Address

McEwan Hall, Teviot Place, EH1

Edinburgh University's plans for this extravagant graduation hall (described in *The Buildings of Scotland* as a 'magnificent petrified blancmange') were considered to be frivolous by the Government and it refused to fund the building. Brewing magnate William McEwan stepped in and contributed £115,000 towards its construction. McEwan specified lavish internal decoration, including panels containing representations of the goddesses of Science, Art and Literature, the Virtues and even a depiction of himself presenting the hall to the University. It was three years before the ornamentation was completed. McEwan was granted the Freedom of Edinburgh in recognition of his gift.

Notable graduates of Edinburgh University include novelists Robert Louis Stevenson, Arthur Conan Doyle (who based the

character of Sherlock Holmes on his medical tutor, Dr Joseph Bell), Walter Scott, John Witherspoon (a signatory of the American Declaration of Independence) and Charles Darwin.

Location	Bristo Square, EH1, west side of square
Map grid	3E
Built	Not known
Cryptic clue	Subtract the last letter of a west country city, a hotel in Paris and an elegant car to find this word

Address

Bristo Square, EH1

I will say it fairly, it grows on me with every year: there are no stars so lovely as Edinburgh street-lamps. When I forget thee, Auld Reekie, may my right hand forget its cunning!

Robert Louis Stevenson

Not far from Edinburgh University's hallowed Medical School, adjacent to Bristo Square, is a bronze plaque that commemorates Dr James Barry. Dr Barry graduated from the school in 1812 and enjoyed a distinguished military career, retiring as the Inspector General of Hospitals, one of the army's most senior medical positions. It was only after Dr Barry died in 1865 that a sensational discovery was made. He was a she! James Miranda Barry had secretly become the first woman in 1812 to study medicine at Edinburgh University. Barry lived in disguise as a man throughout her life because females were not permitted to work as doctors. It was a commonly

held opinion that '…*women are neither physically nor mentally strong enough to cope with the endless medical round…their delicate sensibilities surely equip them to be the handmaids of doctors…*'.

Women had to wait until 1869 before they were allowed to attend medical lectures at Edinburgh University. In response, male students rioted against the presence of females, hustling and preventing them from entering classes.

Location	George IV Bridge, EH1, east side of the street
Map grid	2E
Architect	Reginald Fairlie. Completed by A R Conlon. Panels by Maxwell Allan, James Barr
Built	1938–56 (delayed by World War II)
Style	Classical Modern
Cryptic clue	Read all about Caledonia here

Address

Scotland's largest library traces its origins to 1680 and since then has amassed a unique collection including an 11th century Jerome manuscript bible, a 15th century Gutenberg bible, letters written by Mary, Queen of Scots, and a copy of the National Covenant.

Seven allegorical figures decorate the library's facade and represent the Poetic Muse, History, Justice, Theology, Science, Music and Medicine. The panel in the photograph is one of six that depict the transfer of ideas into the written word.

George IV Bridge was built 1829–32 to improve access from Old Town to the expanding south side of the city. King George IV had visited Edinburgh in 1822, the first monarch to venture north of the border for over 170 years. His memorable visit was master-minded by novelist Walter Scott, and is remembered for its great pageantry and the 'tartanisation' of Edinburgh. Even the King wore a short kilt, but protected his chubby legs from the gusts blowing off the Firth of Forth by donning pink tights. Charitably described as being stout of stature, George IV had a gargantuan

appetite and was once allegedly witnessed by the Duke of Wellington consuming a breakfast that included three steaks, two pigeons, a bottle of wine, two glasses of port, a glass of champagne and a glass of brandy.

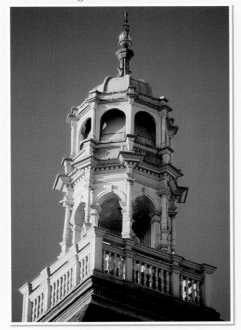

Location	George IV Bridge, EH1, west side of the street
Map grid	2E
Architect	George Washington Browne
Built	1887–90
Style	French Renaissance
Cryptic clue	A principal book depository

Address

Central Library, George IV Bridge, EH1

Edinburgh's Central Library was the country's first Carnegie library – generously funded by industrialist Andrew Carnegie, who was born in Scotland and made his fortune in America.

A surprise awaits those who peek over George IV Bridge – there are several more floors of the library reaching all the way down to Edinburgh's oldest street, the canyon-like Cowgate. Despite being a route along which cattle were driven to market, Cowgate was highly fashionable – '*where the nobility and chief citizens dwell and the greatest in the land have their palaces, where nothing is cheap or mean but all things are magnificent*'. And being a wealthy neighbourhood it was one of Edinburgh's first streets (in the 1670s) to adopt an expensive innovation – glass windows. However, with the advent of New

Town, people with money moved out and by the 19th century Cowgate was a filthy slum and home to some of Edinburgh's poorest citizens.

Location	Castlehill, EH1, south side of the street
Map grid	1D
Architect	Not known
Built	16th century (the sign is 20th century)
Style	Scottish tenement
Cryptic clue	A character in *Macbeth* who says: '*When shall we three meet again, in thunder, lightning, or in rain?*'

Address

The Witchery, Boswell's Court, 352 Castlehill, EH1

Hundreds of alleged witches were burned at the stake outside the Castle gates between 1479 and 1722. The Witchery restaurant is named after this dark period of Edinburgh's history. Witch-hunting was an obsession in Scotland for over two centuries. Witch Prickers were employed to identify those in league with the devil. Pins were stuck into the skin of the accused – those who winced or bled were innocent. However, a notorious pricker called John Kincaid specialised in locating places on the body that felt no pain and released no blood when punctured. He may also have used a device with a retractable spike that did not come into contact with the skin. Using this technique, and being paid per capita, he excelled at finding witches wherever he looked. This gruesome era is alluded to in the restaurant's sign, with the flames and red heart representing the women (and some men) who lost their lives. Many of them were healers who used herbs and unconventional treatments in their craft, but that was enough for them to be suspected of devil-worship. The crown and unicorns refer to the Duke of Gordon

who lived in the tenement when he was Keeper of the Keys to Edinburgh Castle. During the 18th century, the Hell Fire Club met in the building's basement and that explains the red devil motif.

Boswell's Court is named after Dr James Boswell, who lived in the tenement during the 18th century. His nephew, also called James Boswell, was the biographer of Dr Samuel Johnson, who compiled the first dictionary of the English language in 1755.

Location	Castlehill, EH1, south side of the street
Map grid	1D
Architect	Robert Wilson
Built	1896
Style	Scottish Baronial
Cryptic clue	All you ever wanted to know about Scotland's 'water of life'.

Address

Before this building housed the homage to whisky, it was a school for poor children. Victorian philanthropy inspired the Ragged School movement to educate children regardless of their ability to pay.

Whisky is a corruption of *usquebaugh*, from the Scottish Gaelic *uisige beatha*, a translation of the Latin phrase *aqua vitae* – water of life. It has been distilled in Scotland for centuries. As the water of life, it was considered to possess medicinal properties and drunk three times a day despite early whisky being a harsh spirit that bore little relation to today's Scotch. During the days of craft guilds, only barber-surgeons were permitted to sell whisky – for purely medicinal purposes of course! With the discovery of anaesthetics and aspirin still centuries away, it was the nearest thing to a painkiller.

When a barrel of *uisige beatha* was lost and found a couple of years later, the contents were discovered to have mellowed, the flavour developed and the liquid turned a golden colour. From then on,

whisky was left to age in the wood. Today it is big business with Scotch whisky accounting for one fifth of the UK's food and drink exports.

Location	Castlehill, EH1, north side of the street
Map grid	1D
Architect	Not known
Built	16th century, restored 19th century
Style	Scottish tenement
Cryptic clue	A Latin dark chamber and novelty optical invention

Address

Camera Obscura & Outlook Tower, 543–9 Castlehill, EH1

Within this 17th century building is Edinburgh's oldest visitor attraction, a camera obscura and outlook tower. When it opened to the public in 1853, it capitalised on the recently constructed Waverley railway station that made travel much easier and spurred the growth of the city's tourism industry. Victorian tourists came in search of the romantic Edinburgh of Walter Scott's novels and its gothic under-belly (Robert Louis Stevenson's book *The Strange Case of Dr Jekyll and Mr Hyde*, published in 1886, was based on a real-life Edinburgh scoundrel).

The one-storey, red sandstone block next door on Castlehill was formerly a reservoir that held two million gallons of water. It was built in 1849 to supply the wells of Old Town.

Location	Lawnmarket, EH1, north side of the street
Map grid	1D
Architect	Not known
Built	1550
Style	Scottish tenement
Cryptic clue	Victorian Prime Minister and his leather bag

Address

Gladstone's Land is a restored merchant's house dating from 1550, owned for a time by Thomas Gledstanes, a distant relation of Victorian Prime Minister William Gladstone. By the 1930s the building was a condemned slum facing demolition until it was rescued by a private citizen and extensively restored. The ground floor arcade, a feature that was common in 16th century tenements, is a rare survivor.

An unusual aspect of life in Edinburgh's Old Town was that rich and poor lived in such close proximity, sometimes in the same buildings, albeit in domestic circumstances that reflected their wealth. For instance, a blacksmith might live and work in the cellar, then on the ground floor, a trader and his booth in the arcade. On the first floor a lawyer may reside, and above him a merchant, then a widowed aristocrat and so on up the building in an inclining scale of income. Mansions belonging to the aristocracy and clergy were situated in private closes, while menial workers inhabited overcrowded

tenements in the public wynds leading off High Street.

The golden hawk above the door is a visual clue to the one-time owner of the building. In Scotland, another word for this bird of prey is *gled*.

Location	Lawnmarket, EH1, north side of the street
Map grid	1E
Built	1890s
Cryptic clue	Combine armed conflict with a globule of liquid where tennis is played

Address

Wardrop's Court is named after John Wardrop, an Edinburgh merchant who owned a house in this close in 1712. The green dragons date from the 1890s and guard the entrance to the courtyard of restored 17th and 18th century tenements.

Lawnmarket, originally known as Landmarket, was the most fashionable area of Old Town. Here in the widest section of the Royal Mile, a medieval market sold produce from the land – milk, butter, cheese, eggs. On Wednesdays, woollen cloth and a finely woven linen known as lawn could be purchased – this may explain the corruption of the street name from Land to Lawnmarket.

The closes and wynds off the Royal Mile were a secret weapon against armed forces attempting to storm the Castle. Scottish fighters would hide in the darkness of the closes then stream out to attack the invaders, after which they retreated into the warren-like network of wynds and disappeared from the enemy.

Parts of the Royal Mile are 14 feet wider now than when the street was originally laid out. In 1511, the Town Council needed to dispose of a glut of wood so it permitted anyone who attached a new wooden frontage on their building, to extend the property into the street. Wood was also used for 'windows' because glass-making was not introduced to Scotland until the 17th century. To see out or let the light in was simple – holes were cut out of the wooden board.

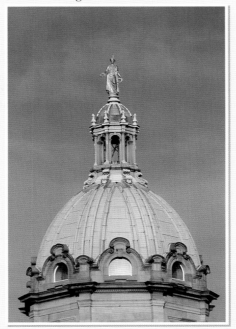

Location	Bank Street, EH1, north side of the street
Map grid	1E
Architect	Robert Reid and Richard Crichton. Remodelled by David Bryce
Built	1806. Remodelled 1864–70
Style	Baroque
Cryptic clue	If Scotland were a river, you would find these on each side

Address

Bank of Scotland, Bank Street, EH1

A statue of Fame stands on top of Britain's oldest clearing bank, established in 1695 by an act of the Scottish Parliament. At the time, Scotland was poor, enduring a turbulent period and uncertain future with its neighbour to the south. Barter or payment in kind was the manner of business in much of rural Scotland. In urban areas, coins were in short supply and not always trusted. The introduction of paper money by the Bank of Scotland in 1696 improved conditions for trade and industry and helped to stabilise the economy.

This site on Bank Street was purchased at a cost of £1,350 for a purpose built company headquarters. A Georgian villa with dome was constructed in 1796. Within 50 years it was too small for the expanding business. New wings were added and the old building was encased in the current Baroque exterior. Statues on the facades represent goddesses and subjects related to commerce. Fame is symbolic of achievement; Prosperity, with an urn and grapes, and Plenty holding

a sheaf of corn in her arm stand on two subsidiary domes. Other statues represent Britannia and her children, Agriculture, Navigation, Commerce and Mechanics.

When Bonnie Prince Charlie marched south in 1745 to proclaim his exiled father as Britain's rightful King (James III), the directors, concerned that civil strife would accompany the Prince's arrival in Edinburgh, stored papers and valuables at the Castle and closed the bank's doors.

Location	Bank Street, EH1, north side of the street
Map grid	1E
Architect	Robert Reid and Richard Crichton. Remodelled by David Bryce
Built	1806. Remodelled 1864–70
Style	Baroque
Cryptic clue	What a plane does when it tips laterally in northern Britain

Address

Bank of Scotland, Bank Street, EH1

First used in 1701 the Bank of Scotland coat of arms consists of a shield bearing St Andrew's Cross surrounded by bezants (gold coins of Byzantium). Justice holding scales, and Plenty with her cornucopia of money flank the shield. The Latin motto '*Tanto Uberior*' means 'so much the more plentiful'. When the bank first opened for business it was in a dim and narrow close off the High Street. A sign bearing the coat of arms and the name of the bank would have helped customers to find their destination. Inside the building, a small museum displays bank notes, coins and their forgeries, and a number of firearms used to protect the bank's money as it was transported through lawless parts of Scotland. Early banknotes were bound in books of up to 200, and individually cut out with a knife or scissors, leaving a rough counterfoil. They were simple in design, bearing little ornamentation but with an intricate script intended to prevent forgeries. If a note looked suspicious, it could be checked against the counterfoil to see if the cut or torn paper edges matched. Forgery was a capital offence and those found guilty could be executed or transported to penal colonies.

The Bank of Scotland first discovered counterfeit notes in 1700. Records indicate that

seven £5 notes had been altered by hand to resemble £50 notes. Forgery prevention measures were introduced, including the engraving of elaborate pictures, the use of specific paper and a contract with just one company to print the notes. Today banknotes contain a number of security featurs including water mark, holograms and embedded metallic strips.

Royal Mile

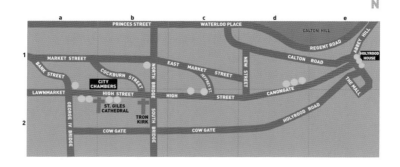

	walking route
	major streets
	location of photograph
	park, square or open space

Royal Mile

Location	High Street, EH1, north side of the street
Map grid	1A
Architect	A J Pitcher, J Wilson Paterson. Justice by Alexander Carrick
Built	1934–7
Style	Neo-Georgian
Cryptic clue	Facing the justice of a county's chief officer

Address

Sheriff Court House, High Court of Justiciary, Lawnmarket, EH1

Three brass bricks laid in the High Street pavement opposite the Court House mark the place where the execution of a murderer named George Bryce was witnessed by 20,000 spectators in 1864. The gibbet was positioned so Bryce faced the Castle as he dropped. It was the last public hanging in Edinburgh.

Underneath the nearby City Chambers (formerly Royal Exchange) lies Mary King's Close, a remarkable historical artefact sealed underground when the Exchange was built on top in the 18th century. Rather than fully demolish the ancient tenements, the builders used them as foundations. Today Mary King's Close is open to visitors, and presents a time capsule of medieval dwellings, all the more atmospheric for being underground. During an outbreak of plague in 1645, the population of Mary King's Close was decimated. A book entitled *Satan's Invisible World Discovered*, written in 1680, described ghostly apparitions in the Close and it was widely believed to be haunted. Could an explanation for the alleged paranormal activity be its proximity to the Nor' Loch? Created in the 15th century as a defensive barrier, Nor' Loch became a noxious sewer that captured all manner of filth thrown or swept down from Old Town.

Decomposing animals and occasionally human corpses contributed to the rich brew of liquid that could barely be described as water, even though it was used for drinking and bathing. Sewer gas rising at night from the polluted swamp combined with Edinburgh's smoky atmosphere may have been mistaken for spectral images.

Location	High Street, EH1, south side of street
Map grid	2A
Craftsmen	J Edgar Boehm, Rowand Anderson, Clark Stanton, Stuart Burnett, W Birnie Rhind.
Built	1887–8
Cryptic clue	Statue where statutes are approved

Buccleuch Statue, Parliament Square, High Street, EH1

Buccleuch was the fifth Duke of that name and earned the honour of this prominent statue for his role in the construction of Granton Harbour, built on land he owned by the Firth of Forth. Ferries from the harbour provided the main transport link north, and in 1850 the world's first train-ferry was established on this route, with railway carriages conveyed across the water by paddle-steamer. The service ceased in 1964 with the construction of the Forth Road Bridge.

Near to the statue, a heart shaped cobblestone design, 'The Heart of Midlothian' marks the location of the 15th century Old Tolbooth prison, demolished in 1817. Here public executions took place, and victim's heads were sometimes displayed on spikes for days afterwards. A local custom of

spitting on the cobbled heart persists from the days when some people would spit on the door of the prison as they walked by.

Location	High Street, EH1, south side of the street
Map grid	2A
Architect	Exterior remodelled 1829 by William Burn
Built	From the 14th century onwards and remodelled in later centuries
Style	Gothic
Cryptic clue	Edinburgh's saintly patron and his church

Address

St Giles Cathedral, High Street, EH1

St Giles is the patron saint of Edinburgh and also of cripples, lepers, tramps and blacksmiths. A church has stood on this site since 1120 but only the top of a column inside survives from that date. The distinctive crown was added in 1495 and symbolises the Kingdom of God.

The cathedral was at the centre of Scottish Protestant Reformation when John Knox became a minister there in 1560. Idolatry was disapproved of and on the feast day of St Giles, when his statue was being carried in the annual procession through town, it was torn down by a mob and thrown into Nor' Loch. The statue was fished out and reinstated in the church. But not for long – it was taken away and burned. In addition, a jewelled reliquary containing St Giles' arm-bone disappeared from the church, never to return. Edinburgh's patron saint was so vehemently out of favour that the town council replaced his image on the burgh arms with that of a thistle.

St Giles Cathedral was partitioned into four and the different areas were used for municipal purposes. These included a law court, a prison for '*harlots and whores*' and the city gallows where a machine known as The Maiden was used to execute more than 150 people. Execution by guillotine is associated with the French Revolution of 1789, but the Scots had invented a device for humane decapitation more than two centuries earlier. The Maiden is on display at Edinburgh's Museum of Scotland on Chambers Street.

Location	High Street, EH1, south side of the street
Map grid	2B
Architect	Sydney Mitchell
Built	1885
Cryptic clue	X market's the spot

Mercat Cross, High Street, EH1

A mercat (or market) cross has stood on or near this site since at least 1365. Originally it was in the middle of the High Street. It represented the centre of the town and was an important symbol. Here merchants gathered to talk business, Royal Proclamations and official announcements were made and public executions carried out. In 1755, it was dismantled as a precautionary measure a decade after Bonnie Prince Charlie stood upon it and proclaimed his father as the rightful monarch. Local Member of Parliament and Prime Minister, William Gladstone donated the funds to build the cross in 1885.

A unicorn traditionally signifies purity and is an emblem of Scotland. St. Andrew's Cross was adopted as the national symbol in AD 735.

Location	High Street, EH1, south side of the street
Map grid	2B
Architect	Sydney Mitchell
Built	1885
Cryptic clue	Where to hear the proclaimers

Address

Mercat Cross, High Street, EH1

Several coats of arms decorate the cross's octagonal base, including those of the city of Edinburgh, the arms of Scotland, England and Ireland, the burgh of Canongate and, in the photograph, the seal of the Port of Leith depicting the Virgin and Child.

To announce the news or read a proclamation, town officials and heralds stood on top of the base. Thousands of people would cram into the vicinity and listen. Since 1603, when the Scottish and English monarchies were united, national news has traditionally been proclaimed three days after London, that being the time it took for a horse rider to complete the journey from the south. Royal Proclamations were composed in flowery language and not known for their brevity. This is a mere fragment of the announcement made at the Mercat Cross for the accession of a new King, Charles II in 1684:

And for testification whereof, we here, in presence of the Almighty God, and a great number of His Majesty's faithful people, of all estates and qualities, who are assisting with us, at

this solemn publication of our due, humble and faithful acknowledgement of his supreme sovereign authority, at the Mercat Cross of the City of Edinburgh, declare and publish, that our said sovereign lord, by the goodness and providence of Almighty God, is of Scotland, England, France and Ireland, and Dominions there-unto belonging, the most potent, mighty, and undoubted King.

Location	High Street, EH1, south side of the street
Map grid	2B
Cryptic clue	If the answer to the joke is 'dam' what is the question? (Solution overleaf)

Address

Old Fishmarket Close, High Street, EH1

Old Fishmarket Close, first recorded in 1592, was named after the fish market that traded within its confines. Poultry was also on sale and shoppers could purchase '*partrikis, pluuaris, capons, conyngis, chekinnis and all uther wyld fowls and tame*'. The aroma of discarded rotting fish and meat would have combined with the overpowering stench of Old Town and made it even more abominable. Legend has it that those travelling to Edinburgh could smell it from miles away. Lavender and rose petals were used in vast quantities to perfume the houses but nothing could compete with the town's malodorous air.

In 1824 a fire destroyed much of the High Street including Old Fishmarket Close, with great loss of life. As a result, the world's first municipal fire service, Edinburgh Fire Engine Establishment was founded.

Cryptic clue answer: What did the fish say when it swam into a concrete wall?

Location	North Bridge, EH1, west side of the street
Map grid	1B
Architect	Dunn & Findlay
Built	1899–1902
Style	Baroque
Cryptic clue	There was an Englishman, an Irishman and a ???

Address

Scotsman Hotel, 20 North Bridge, EH1

Today this building is a hotel, but it was formerly the head office of Scotland's national newspaper, *The Scotsman*. The location was chosen for its proximity to Waverley station. A railway siding led to the Market Street entrance and newspapers were loaded directly onto trains, literally hot off the press. Staff upstairs knew if the presses were printing because the entire building shook.

Only *The Scotsman's* proprietor and senior executives were permitted to enter the building through what is now the hotel entrance – all other staff used a door in Market Street four storeys below. The executives also had exclusive use of a grand Sicilian marble stairway, roped off to lesser beings. However, 11 November was special, each year employees were allowed to use this staircase to assemble for a two-minute silence to mark the armistice of World War I.

When the newspaper moved to new premises in 2000 the building was transformed into the current hotel. Guests can sleep in bedrooms that were formerly editorial and executive offices, some retaining the original wood panelling. A brasserie is located in the paper's main lobby and public

reading room, and a door at the back of the restaurant leads to the Sicilian marble staircase so you can walk down it pretending to be a newspaper magnate.

Location	High Street, EH1, north side of the street
Map grid	2C
Architect	Not known
Built	Early 16th century
Style	Originally medieval
Cryptic clue	A dwelling – rhymes with box and less than two

Address

Known as the father of Protestant Reformation in Scotland, John Knox advocated a style of worship that was plain and puritanical. Although the house on High Street is named after Knox, there is no evidence that he lived in it.

First mentioned in records in 1525 when it was a medieval two-storey house, it followed the pattern of other Old Town buildings and extra levels were built on top. Like many houses of its time, this one has projecting upper storeys to create more space – a practice known as 'jetting'.

The figure above the sundial in the photograph resembles John Knox but it is Moses. He is pointing to a cloud inscribed 'God' in Greek, Latin and English.

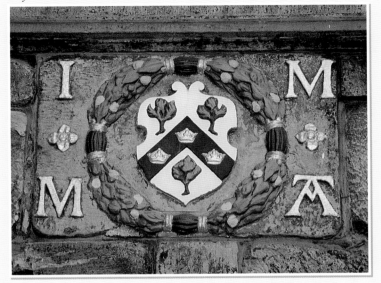

Location	High Street, EH1, north side of the street
Map grid	2C
Architect	Not known
Built	Early 16th century
Style	Originally medieval
Cryptic clue	Survivors of bad experiences are graduates of this hard school

John Knox House, 45 High Street, EH1

JM and MA are the initials of James Mosman and Mariotta
Arres who owned this house in the mid-16th century. Mosman
was a goldsmith and master of the mint. His father John, also
a goldsmith, had refashioned the Crown of Scotland into its
present form – a base made from Scottish gold, encrusted with
precious stones and freshwater pearls from Scotland's rivers. A
sword and sceptre completes the 'Honours of Scotland', the
country's sovereign regalia.

To the west of John Knox House is Moubray House, the oldest
occupied building in Edinburgh, built in 1477. Outside is a
square stone structure – Netherbow Well where Edinburgh
citizens would have queued up to collect fresh water.

There were several wells in Old Town and some were still in
use in the 1930s. Porters, known as water caddies (from the
French word, *cadet*), could be hired to carry pails of water up

to tenement flats. The job
of caddy lives on, only
now it is on the golf
course.

Location	High Street, EH1, north side of the street
Map grid	2C
Architect	Not known
Built	Mid-19th century
Style	Scottish tenement
Cryptic clue	Drink from a French cup in this pub

Address

Go, fetch to me a pint o' wine
And fill it in a silver tassie
That I may drink before I go
A service to my bonie lassie!

A silver tassie in poet Robert Burn's song is a drinking goblet. Tass or tassie is a Scottish-Franco term from *tasse*, the French word for cup.

Previously this pub was called the Royal Archer and the figure above the door represents a member of the Royal Company of Archers. This organisation functions as the monarch's guard in Scotland, although nowadays for ceremonial purposes only. A Royal Archer bodyguard may conjure images of medieval derring-do but the role of protection dates only from 1822 and the grand pageant that

surrounded King George IV's visit to Edinburgh. The Company was founded in 1676 as a private archery club and members have the right to '*perpetual access to all public butts, plains and pasturages legally allotted for shooting arrows*'. In exchange for these privileges the Company is required to present three arrows to the Sovereign. Today, the Royal Company of Archers' role is to attend state and ceremonial occasions in Scotland when required by the monarch.

Location	Canongate, EH8, north side of the street
Map grid	1D
Architect	Not known
Built	1677 and restored 1880s
Style	Scottish tenement
Cryptic clue	Where the Old and New Testaments live

Address

Known as Bible Land because of text from psalm 133 carved on the shield above the door, this building, originally called Shoemakers Hall, was purchased in 1677 by the Guild of Cordwainers of the Canongate. Cordwainer (or Cordiner) is a term for a shoemaker – the word derives from the use of goat leather imported from Cordoba in Spain. Also on the shield is the emblem of the guild, a crowned shoemaker's rounding knife flanked by cherubs.

Canongate was founded in 1143 as a burgh independent from Edinburgh. Although living conditions were much more salubrious than in Edinburgh, the downside was that buildings outside the town walls were the first to be ransacked whenever the enemy invaded. This danger passed in 1707 with the Act

of Union between Scotland and England. Moray House (diagonally opposite Bible Land) was supposed to be the location for the signing of this momentous treaty but rioters who opposed the Union forced the signatories to seek refuge in an anonymous High Street cellar where the Act was inscribed.

Location	Canongate, EH8, north side of the street
Map grid	1D
Architect	Restored by Robert Morham
Built	1591 and restored 1875. Clock 1884
Style	Scottish Baronial
Cryptic clue	For whom the booth tolls

Address

Canongate Tolbooth, Canongate, EH8

Tolbooth is the oldest building in Canongate and was built as the administrative centre of the burgh, with council chambers and courtrooms upstairs and a jail below. Here visitors entering Edinburgh paid a toll to pass through the burgh gates. During curfew hours these gates were bolted and citizens who were locked out had to pay to enter – a penny for ordinary people, but twice that for the '*best of the town*'.

Canongate evolved as the Court Quarter and it was lined with the large mansions of nobles who served the Sovereign at the Palace of Holyroodhouse. When the monarchies of Scotland and England were combined in 1603, King James VI moved to London to be crowned James I of England. The Royal Court accompanied him and Canongate entered a period of decline.

Royal Mile 13

Location	Canongate, EH8, north side of the street
Map grid	1D
Architect	James Smith
Built	1688–91
Style	A combination of classical and Baroque
Cryptic clue	Poor as a ?? mouse

Canongate Kirk, Canongate, EH8

Canongate Kirk was built as the parish church of the burgh
after Holyrood Abbey was destroyed by a Protestant mob.
Decorating the Kirk facade are the coats of arms of Thomas
Moodie, who paid for the church construction, and those of
King William III. On the pinnacle, a golden stag head
symbolises the miracle that led to the founding of Holyrood
Abbey. It has been an element of the Abbey Seal since 1453.

The name Canongate derives from the route taken by
Augustinian canons from Holyrood Abbey to the Edinburgh
town gate.

Location	Abbey Strand and Horse Wynd, EH8
Map grid	1E
Architect	Archibald Simpson and John Henderson. Gallery by Benjamin Tindall
Built	1846–50. Gallery 1999–2002
Style	Victorian
Cryptic clue	A man in female attire might play to this

Address

Inaugurated during Queen Elizabeth II's Jubilee celebrations in 2002, the gallery displays a selection of art, jewellery and furniture from the Royal Collection. It occupies the shells of a 19th-century church and a charity school. Over the entrance, Scotland's heraldic lion welcomes visitors.

Abbey Strand represents the boundary of the Girth of Holyrood, Scotland's largest sanctuary. A letter 'S' marked in bronze on the road indicates the perimeter. Sanctuary (a protection from civil law traditionally afforded by religious establishments) was established at Holyrood in the 12th century under a charter granted by King David I. Those claiming asylum had to make a formal application to the Bailie of Holyrood for the '*benefit and privilege*' of sanctuary. If haven was granted, the asylum seekers paid a booking fee, and '*letters of protection*' were issued. This allowed them to live in the Girth of Holyrood, free from arrest because it was not under the jurisdiction of Canongate or Edinburgh. Refugees

were known as 'Abbey Lairds' and could leave the sanctuary at midnight on a Saturday and spend the following day without fear of arrest because legal proceedings were forbidden on a Sunday. Debtors in particular took advantage of Holyrood's sanctuary until 1880 when mandatory imprisonment for insolvency was abolished. Holyrood's sanctuary has never been formally annulled though whether traffic wardens would recognise it for delinquent car parking is doubtful.

Location	Abbey Strand, EH8, south side of the street
Map grid	1E
Built	19th century
Style	Victorian
Cryptic clue	If the answer to the joke is 'play leapfrog', what is the question? (Solution overleaf)

Address

Abbey Strand, EH8

King James V was the first Scottish monarch to include a unicorn in the royal coat of arms. In addition to symbolising purity, the unicorn also has a political dimension in the ancient hostilities between Scotland and England, for the unicorn is also known for its struggle with the lion, and the lion is a symbol of England.

In Edmund Spenser's poem, *The Faerie Queen* (composed in the 1590s), he wrote '*the lyon, whose imperial power a proud rebellious unicorn defies*'. In order to defeat his rival, the lion employed trickery by stepping aside at the last moment when the unicorn charged. Unable to stop, the unicorn slammed into a tree and its horn stuck tight, leaving the lion safe.

When James VI united the thrones of Scotland and England in 1603, his coat of arms displayed both the unicorn and the lion. This has been the heraldic symbol of the monarch ever since.

Cryptic clue answer: What does a wise person never do with a unicorn?

Location   Abbey Strand, EH8, east end of the street
Map grid   1E
Cryptic clue   A palatial, movable barrier

Address

Palace of Holyroodhouse, EH8 (entry gates)

Great dramas of state have been played out over the centuries at Holyroodhouse. Mary Queen of Scots spent time here during her turbulent reign and when she was six months pregnant with the future King James VI, witnessed the murder of her personal secretary David Rizzio by conspirators seeking to undermine her. Charles I was crowned King of Scotland at Holyroodhouse. In 1745, Bonnie Prince Charlie briefly held court at the Palace during his unsuccessful attempt to claim the throne for his father. For the next few decades, the structure of the empty building deteriorated until it was restored for the visit of King George IV in 1822. He established it as the official royal residence in Scotland and every monarch since has visited on a regular basis.

New Town

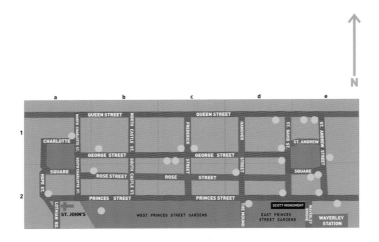

a   b   c   d   e

QUEEN STREET   QUEEN STREET

NORTH CHARLOTTE ST.
NORTH CASTLE ST.
FREDERICK STREET
HANOVER STREET
ST. DAVID ST.
ST. ANDREW STREET

CHARLOTTE

GEORGE STREET   GEORGE STREET

SOUTH CHARLOTTE ST.
SOUTH CASTLE ST.

SQUARE

HOPE ST.

ST. ANDREW
SQUARE

ROSE STREET   ROSE   STREET

PRINCES   STREET   PRINCES STREET

LOTHIAN RD.

ST. JOHN'S

THE MOUND

SCOTT MONUMENT

WEST PRINCES STREET GARDENS

EAST PRINCES
STREET GARDENS

WAVERLEY BRIDGE

WAVERLEY
STATION

1

2

N

---

walking route

major streets

location of photograph

park, square or open space

New Town

Location	Princes Street, EH2, south side of the street
Map grid	2E
Architect	William Hamilton Beattie
Built	1902
Style	16th century Franco-German
Cryptic clue	Highland castle with royal connections

Address

Balmoral Hotel, 1 Princes Street, EH2

Robert Louis Stevenson described the North Bridge corner of the
Balmoral Hotel as '*the high altar in this northern temple of winds*'. Afternoon
tea in the hotel's Victorian Palm Court is a great escape from the
windiest spot in town.

The Balmoral was originally called the North British and it was built as a
grand hotel to serve Waverley railway station. Luxury extended to the
smallest furnishings – japanned dishes to capture drips from fire
hydrants and thermometers in lacquered cases to measure the
temperature of bath water.

On New Year's Eve, the Balmoral's clock is the focus for thousands of
Hogmanay revellers on Princes Street when the countdown to midnight
begins. This is the only time the clock registers accurate Greenwich

Mean Time. On all other days it is two minutes
fast so people running late for the train will
arrive with time to spare. The clock tower is an
Edinburgh landmark and its situation has made
it the second most photographed location in
the city after the Castle.

Waverley is unique for being the only railway
station in Britain named after a novel (by Walter
Scott). British Rail planned to rename it in the
1990s but opposition to change was too strong.

Location	Princes Street, EH2, north side of the street
Map grid	2E
Architect	John J Burnet
Built	1906–10
Style	Baroque
Cryptic clue	A top shop with principles

Address

Princes Street's spectacular panorama was under threat from developers clamouring to build on the Gardens from the time they were laid out. Legal battles raged but the conservationists won when a Statute of Parliament was passed in 1816 to protect in perpetuity the public open space. With the exception of the museums and Scott Monument, no building has been permitted since.

The street was originally to be named after Edinburgh's patron saint, St Giles, but it was changed when King George III objected. To him, St Giles was already a familiar moniker but as the name of a rat-infested slum and former leper colony in London.

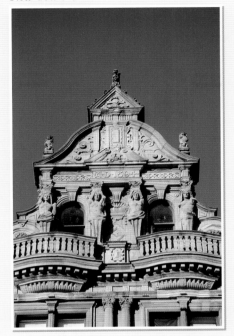

Location	Princes Street, EH2, north side of the street
Map grid	2D
Architect	William Hamilton Beattie
Built	1893–5
Style	French Renaissance
Cryptic clue	Shares a surname (plural) with vaccination pioneer

Jenners, 48 Princes Street, EH2

Jenners has the distinction of being the world's first department store. Founded in humble circumstances, Charles Jenner and his partner Charles Kennington took the lease on a small Princes Street shop, rent £150 per annum, and opened for business in 1838. An advertisement to herald the new venture read:

> **Kennington & Jenner**
> *Will open their new establishment on Tuesday 1st May with every prevailing British and Parisian fashion, in silks, shawls, fancy dresses, ribbons, lace, hosiery, and every description of linen drapery and haberdashery.*

After Mr Kennington died, the business was renamed Jenners. The original store was destroyed by fire in 1892 but work began immediately on a new shop. Charles Jenner died before the current building was completed but he had taken a great interest in the project. In his will he bequeathed £8,000 for the provision

of caryatids to be carved into the shop's exterior. These symbolised the women staff and customers who had always supported the business. Charles Jenner described Edinburgh women as '*the best dressed ladies in the Kingdom*'.

The new store was well ahead of its time with hydraulic lifts, lavish electrical lighting (electricity had just been installed in Edinburgh) and air-conditioning. By 2pm on reopening day, 25,000 people had inspected the splendid new emporium.

Location	Hanover Street, EH2, west side of the street
Map grid	2D
Architect	David Bryce Junior
Built	1865–6
Style	Classical
Cryptic clue	Which merchant said '*Nature hath framed strange fellows in her time*'?
	(Answer overleaf)

Address

The Merchants Hall, 22 Hanover Street, EH2

Granted a charter by King Charles II in 1681, the original purpose of the Merchant Company was to protect trading rights in Edinburgh. Merchants had wealth and power and members of the guild sat on the town council, giving them great influence.

The coat of arms in the photograph is symbolic of the Company's mercantile origins. Edinburgh's history of export trade is alluded to by the sailing ship, and the Latin phrase *Terraque Marique* – 'by land and by sea' is depicted by two sea unicorns, half sea and half land creatures.

Hanover Street is named after the House of Hanover that reigned in Britain from King George I in 1714 until 1837 when Queen Victoria ascended the throne. After World War I when anti-German feeling was high, there were calls to replace the Teutonic street name. Handover Street was suggested as

an alternative but the original moniker has remained.

Cryptic clue answer: Antonio, *The Merchant of Venice* – act 1, scene 1.

Location	The Mound, EH2, east side of the street
Map grid	2D
Architect	William Playfair
Built	1822–6 and 1831–6
Style	Classical
Cryptic clue	Scotland's regal society for advancing arts

Address

Royal Scottish Academy, The Mound, EH2

'Athens of the North' is how architect James Stuart described Edinburgh in the 18th century with its abundance of Graeco-Roman buildings. The father of Athenian Edinburgh is architect William Playfair, who whilst not well-known outside Scotland, left his legacy in some of the city's major buildings, for instance the City Observatory on Calton Hill.

The Academy is on a street called The Mound, a thoroughfare that owes its origin to a tailor named George Boyd. When Nor' Loch was still in place, rather than walk the long way round from Old Town to visit his clients in New Town, Boyd laid a trail of planks and stones across the swampy loch. 'Geordie Boyd's Mud Brig' became a much-used unofficial path. When Nor' Loch was drained, it made sense to build a proper route to Princes Street and the city council assumed responsibility for Geordie's creation. Some two million cartloads of soil and rock excavated during the construction of New Town were dumped to create The Mound.

In 1959, the Weather Blanket was laid under The Mound. This consisted of 47 miles of electric cable embedded in the road surface to act as a heating element and prevent ice forming so traffic could climb the slope. It was decommissioned in 1977 because of heavy repair costs.

Location	West Princes Street Gardens, EH2, west end of gardens
Map grid	2B
Architect	Jean-Baptiste Jales Klagman
Built	1862
Cryptic clue	Land-locked mermaids find artificial ornamental solace

Address

Ross Fountain, West Princes Street Gardens, EH2

'Grossly indecent and disgusting, insulting and offensive to the moral feelings of the community and disgraceful to the city' were the comments of the Dean of a nearby church when the Ross Fountain was installed in Princes Street Gardens. Daniel Ross, an Edinburgh gunsmith, purchased the sculpture in France and donated it to the city. It was delivered to the port of Leith in 122 pieces and assembled in 1872. Today the fountain is listed as a structure of historic importance.

Location	West Princes Street Gardens, EH2
Map grid	2B
Architect	Jean-Baptiste Jales Klagman
Built	1862
Cryptic clue	What an Antarctic ice sheet and a singing goddess of the hunt have in common

Address

Ross Fountain, West Princes Street Gardens, EH2

Princes Street Gardens were laid out after the Nor' Loch was drained. The loch had been artificially created as a defensive barrier during the reign of King James IV (1437–1513). James ordered the first town wall to be built, with Nor' Loch to the north of it. The Wellhouse Tower, by the foot of Castle rock is a fragment of the wall. The Wellhouse protected a spring known as St Margaret's Well that was used to supply the Castle with water hauled up the rock face in buckets on a rope.

Location	Rose Street, EH2, north side of the street
Map grid	2B
Architect	Not known
Built	18th century
Style	Georgian
Cryptic clue	Filthy Richard (diminutive)

Address

Dirty Dick's, 159 Rose Street, EH2

Rose Street was lined with taverns by the 19th century, despite New Town being officially 'dry'. Only a handful of them remain today, and its rakish reputation has waned despite its popularity for pub-crawls along the 'Amber Mile'.

Named to symbolise the Act of Union (the rose is an emblem of England), with nearby Thistle Street representing Scotland, the street was built to accommodate artisans and tradesmen who serviced the large houses of George and Princes Streets.

Dirty Dick's commemorates a scruffy character who often followed horse-drawn delivery wagons and picked up manure droppings from the street. 'Where there's muck there's brass' was true in Dirty Dick's case. According to legend, poor down-

at-heel Dick died without knowing he had inherited a fortune from his recently deceased mother.

Location	George Street, EH2, north side of the street
Map grid	1B
Architect	Auldjo, Jamieson, Arnott
Built	Early 20th century
Style	Classical Greek/French and Italian Renaissance
Cryptic clue	A country's church

Address

Church of Scotland, 121 George Street, EH2

Since 1958, the Burning Bush emblem has been the official logo of the Church of Scotland but its use goes back to 1691 when a printer named George Mossman used the illustration on the title page of a major church publication. The image symbolises the chapter in the Old Testament Book of Exodus when Moses came upon a burning bush:

> *And the angel of the Lord appeared unto him in a flame of fire out of the midst of a bush and he looked, and behold the bush burned with fire and the bush was not consumed.*

The Latin phrase '*nec tamen consumebatur*' means 'burning but not consumed'.

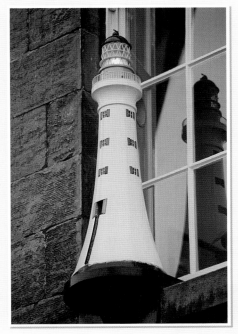

Location	George Street, EH2, south side of the street
Map grid	1C
Architect	Claude Cleghorn
Built	1786
Style	Georgian
Cryptic clue	Officers in charge of the night-time mariners' guides

Address

Commissioners of Northern Lighthouses, 82–84 George Street, EH2

Day and night, this ornamental lighthouse flashes its beacon of warning just as full-sized ones do in treacherous waters off the British coast.

Established in 1786 by an Act of Parliament, the Northern Lighthouse Board is responsible for the lighthouses, buoys and beacons throughout Scotland, its adjacent seas and islands and the Isle of Man. Scotland has a total of 201 lighthouses with names such as Point of Winkie, Barrel of Butter and Butt of Lewis. In the care of the Commissioners were 18 lighthouses built by civil engineer Robert Stevenson whose grandson was the celebrated writer, Robert Louis Stevenson.

Gone are the days when live-in lighthouse keepers braved inclement weather to ensure the beacon was lit. The final manned lighthouse was automated in 1998.

Location	George Street, EH2, south side of the street
Map grid	1C
Architect	John J Burnet. Refurbished by Hugh Martin Partnership 2000–2
Built	1903–7
Style	Baroque
Cryptic clue	A patron saint + one Summertime composer + two Bushes + six British kings x 8

Address

80 George Street, EH2

This Baroque giant is an example of Victorian urban renewal – it replaced two understated Georgian terraced houses. 80 George Street was built as a cooperative department store called the Professional & Civil Service Supply Association. Architect John J Burnet had trained at the École des Beaux-Arts in Paris and the building's colossal size and ornamentation are reminiscent of the Beaux-Arts style.

Throughout its life, the building has undergone significant internal change, with art deco additions in 1936 and gutted interiors during conversion to office use in the 1970s. The building was granted Grade A listed status and was restored to its Baroque distinction by the Hugh Martin Partnership.

George Street was designed to be wide enough for a carriage and four horses to turn round in. Named in honour of King George III, the street was the grandest thoroughfare in New Town and links two squares – St Andrew Square, after Scotland's patron saint, and Charlotte Square for the king's wife, Charlotte of Mecklenburg-Strelitz.

Location	George Street, EH2
Map grid	1C
Architect	T P Marwick
Built	1908
Style	Baroque
Cryptic clue	Days of the week x commandments + what some call the loneliest number

Address

71 George Street, EH2

New Town was built on a plateau known as Barefoot Parks and George Street runs along its spine, Lang Dykes. Architect James Craig dedicated his final plan for New Town to King George III and named several streets after members of the royal family. Frederick Street, laid out in 1790, commemorates the king's father, Prince Frederick. Known as 'Poor Fred', he was allegedly never on good terms with his own father King George II and mother Queen Caroline. As heir to the throne, Frederick surrounded himself with a coterie of Members of Parliament and the King saw this as opposition. Relations, already cool between father and son, deteriorated. Whether Frederick's mother Caroline truly referred to her son as '*the greatest ass, the greatest liar, the greatest canaille and the greatest beast in the whole world and we heartily wish he was out of it*', as

some reports suggest, he was not a favourite. Poor Fred died suddenly aged 44, outlived by his father.

Location	George Street, EH2
Map grid	1C
Architect	George Washington Browne and J M Dick Peddie
Built	1905
Style	French Renaissance
Cryptic clue	Number divisible by 23 that reads the same way upside down

Address

69 George Street, EH2

69 George Street was formerly a branch of the British Linen Bank. Established by Royal Charter in 1746 to promote Scottish linen, the British Linen Company developed banking services for its clients all over Scotland, thus pioneering the concept of a bank branch network.

Unlike most countries in the world, the issue of banknotes in Britain is not restricted to the nation's central bank. Today, the Bank of Scotland, the Royal Bank of Scotland and the Clydesdale Bank print notes. Until the 1950s the British Linen Bank was in that group. Although the company no longer operates as a personal banker, its merchant division still trades as a subsidiary of the Bank of Scotland.

Banks that issue notes are also responsible for disposing of currency at the end of its life cycle. Paper money was formerly incinerated under strict security but nowadays notes are

 shredded and the paper is recycled.

Location	George Street, EH2, north side of the street
Map grid	1D
Architect	Frieze by Gerald Laing
Built	1975
Style	Modern
Cryptic clue	Nothing Standard about the Life of this frieze

Address

Standard Life Investments, 1 George Street, EH2

Be prepared! That is the meaning behind the story of the Wise And Foolish Virgins who feature in this frieze. Jesus told the parable to his disciples and the message was to prepare for the Second Coming. Ten young maidens were invited to a wedding party. As darkness fell, five of them stored extra oil for their lamps but the others did not bother. Later that night when the bridegroom arrived the girls went to greet him. The wise ones with enough oil to light the way were able to join the celebrations, but the foolish girls with no fuel were forced to stay at home.

The photograph represents the wise virgins, organised and carefree. Next to them on the frieze, but out of shot, are five glum maidens who missed out on a great night and all because

they had no savings – a fitting metaphor for a company in the business of financial investments. Gerald Laing's frieze of 1975 is a more modern version of the 1839 rendition in the pediment above the company's entrance next door.

Location	St Andrew Square, EH2, southwest corner
Map grid	1D
Architect	L Grahame Thomson & Frank J Connell. Bronze figures by Alexander Carrick
Built	1938–40
Style	Art deco
Cryptic clue	Construction related to financial assets or primary city

Address

Capital Building, 13 St Andrew Square, EH2

Standing guard above the entrance are two groups of statues that represent Insurance and Security. They symbolise the building's first tenant, Caledonian Insurance Company, founded by a disgruntled Edinburgh merchant who was badly treated by an insurer. The London-based company refused to pay up when the merchant's premises were destroyed by fire, because he had been one day late paying for the annual policy.

Initially Caledonian Insurance Company dealt only in fire coverage, and throughout Edinburgh copperplates bearing the name and badge of the firm began to appear on the walls of buildings. These were known as 'fire-marks'. Until 1824, there was no municipal fire brigade in Edinburgh. In the case of a conflagration, a corps of 14 firefighters employed by

 Caledonian Insurance went to tackle blazes in buildings that bore their company fire-mark.

Location	St Andrew Square, EH2, southwest corner
Map grid	1D
Architect	L Grahame Thomson and Frank J Connell
Built	1938–40
Style	Art deco
Cryptic clue	Unlucky for some

Address

Coats of arms are not just company logos, they act as symbolic mission statements, a signal to customers about what they should expect from that particular business. In the case of the Caledonian Insurance Company, the message on its coat of arms suggested a trustworthy company with high ideals.

The lion represents dauntless courage. An eagle portrays nobility, strength and bravery. When the eagle's wings are spread, as in this case, it signifies protection. A helmet means wisdom and security, while the shield stands for the defender. St Andrew's Cross represents Scotland and also resolution. A thistle is the emblem of Scotland and has its own legend – the story of Viking invaders who chanced upon a band of sleeping Scottish warriors. When one of the Vikings trod on a thistle he cried out in pain and alerted the Scots who were able to defeat the raiders. From then on, the barbed plant was known as the Guardian Thistle.

'Providemus' is a Latin term that translates as 'we shall be seeing' and is related to forethought, foresight and caution.

Location	St Andrew Square, EH2, south side of the square
Map grid	2E
Architect	Burnet, Son & Dick
Built	1923–5
Style	Baroque
Cryptic clue	The number of a crowd if two is company

Address

3 St Andrew Square, EH2

St Andrew Square can be located from a distance by looking Up for a 150-foot pillar based on Trajan's Column in Rome. On its top stands a statue of 'Harry the Ninth, the uncrowned king of Scotland' as Henry Dundas was dubbed. Described in 1800 as the '*absolute dictator in Scotland*', Dundas wielded enormous power as the Central Government's enforcer north of the border.

When the Square was laid out, the cost of houses ranged from £1,800 to £5,000. Today property values are immense and St Andrew Square contains such wealthy financial and insurance institutions that their combined assets are reputed to make this the richest square in Europe.

St Andrew was a disciple of Jesus and was crucified by the Romans as punishment for his Christian beliefs. According to legend, Andrew claimed to be unworthy of dying on the same shaped cross as Christ and chose a diagonal one instead. The

cross, named after St Andrew is also known as the Saltire.

Myth surrounds the adoption of the Saltire as Scotland's flag. One tale tells of an 8th-century king, Angus, who dreamt that St Andrew assured him of great victory over the rival King of Northumbria. Later in battle, Angus saw a white diagonal cross appear in the blue sky. His troops were victorious and from then on, they carried banners bearing a white cross on a blue background.

Location	St Andrew Square, EH2, south side of the square
Map grid	2E
Architect	Alfred Waterhouse
Built	1892–5
Style	French Renaissance
Cryptic clue	The favourite number of a self-centred person

Address

Prudence is one of the Seven Heavenly Virtues with Faith, Hope, Charity, Fortitude, Justice and Temperance. She has been the symbol of Prudential (formerly based at 1 St Andrew Square) since 1848. With her sound judgement, common sense and caution she embodies ideal qualities for a company in the business of financial services.

Down as alleyway opposite the statue of Prudence is the Café Royal (look out for the lobster sign). Opened in 1863 as a hotel, this building is a survivor. It's a time capsule and has been used as a period location in films such as *Chariots of Fire*. Doulton tiles depicting renowned inventors decorate the walls and, in the Oyster Bar, stained-glass windows portray men engaged in popular Victorian sports.

Woolworth's eyed the Café Royal for purchase and demolition in the 1960s so they could build a car park for their Princes Street store. The public outcry was so great that the Café was granted Grade A listed status. Woolworth's no longer trades in Princes Street, but the Café Royal remains in its original site.

Location	St Andrew Square, EH2, east side of the square
Map grid	1E
Architect	David Bryce
Built	1846
Style	Classical
Cryptic clue	What you would break if you were gambling in Mid Lothian's version of Monte Carlo

Address

Bank of Scotland, 38 St Andrew Square, EH2

A hint of Imperial Rome stands in St Andrew Square with the Bank of Scotland's colossal edifice. The statues represent Navigation, Commerce, Manufacture, Art, Science and Agriculture. Inside is a spectacular banking hall that is covered by an engraved glass dome. On the walls are medallions celebrating eminent Scots including economist Adam Smith, author Walter Scott and inventor James Watt. Hidden under the carpet are the original decorative Minton floor tiles.

St Andrew Square was conceived as a mirror image of Charlotte Square at the opposite end of George Street. The Church of St Andrew was to have stood next to what is now the Bank of Scotland. The plan was thwarted when Member of Parliament Laurence Dundas used his influence to buy the land for his mansion, Dundas House. St Andrew's Church was relegated to a site at the end of George Street and the symmetrical harmony of New Town's architectural vision was altered. Dundas House was purchased by the Royal Bank of Scotland and like its

neighbour, has a stunning banking hall. In its early days, the Royal Bank had the honour of designing Scotland's banknotes. For the first years, notes were printed in black and white and on one side only, but in 1777 the Royal Bank was the first in Europe to use colour in its currency as an anti-forgery measure. It had previously pioneered another financial service – in 1728, it issued the world's first overdraft to a merchant named William Hog, permitting him to withdraw £1,000 (over £60,000 in today's money) more than he had in his account.

Location	St Andrew Street, EH2, west side of the street
Map grid	1E
Architect	Rowand Anderson
Built	1885–90
Style	Gothic revival
Cryptic clue	Scottish Portrait of a Lady, and also a king, queen, politician, writer, philosopher, architect

Address

Scottish Portrait Gallery, 1 Queen Street, EH2

Mary, Queen of Scots is flanked in the photograph by Bishop John Leslie, her ardent supporter, and by royal adviser William Maitland. Mary ruled Scotland during a fractious period, exacerbated by her Catholicism, in the time of Protestant Reformation. Hostile Scottish nobles rose against Mary and demanded her abdication. She fled to England but was imprisoned for 19 years by Queen Elizabeth, then executed because of the suspicion that she was the figurehead of an uprising against the English monarch.

Like many Victorian monuments, the facade of the Scottish Portrait Gallery is rich in symbolism with statues representing Scotland, History, Industry, Religion, Fine Arts, Poetry, Painting, the Sciences and War and Peace. Scottish heroes

such as Robert the Bruce and figures of great historical importance, for instance John Knox, are also depicted in the building's red Dumfriesshire sandstone.

Location	Queen Street, EH2, south side of the street
Map grid	1E
Cryptic clue	Lighting the street of an alpha female

Address

Before electricity was introduced to Edinburgh, streetlamps were fuelled by gas. Municipal lighting was limited and those who could afford it hired a linkboy to walk ahead of them carrying a flare to light the way. Ornate flame snuffers in the shape of a snake's head were dotted about New Town – the linkboy inserted the flare into the snake's mouth to extinguish it and save fuel.

Queen Street has altered little since it was laid out in the 1760s, built as a mirror image of the original Princes Street with buildings on one side only and landscaped gardens opposite. Queen Street, named after the consort of King George III, contains Edinburgh's longest stretch of 18th-century architecture.

Location	Queen Street, EH2, south side of the street
Map grid	1D
Architect	Thomas Hamilton
Built	1844
Style	Classical
Cryptic clue	A dose of doctors

Address

Royal College of Physicians, 9–10 Queen Street, EH2

On the wall behind the ornate lamp is the Staff of Aesculapius around which a serpent is coiled. The motif represents the medical profession and is a symbol of health and wisdom. In Greek mythology, Aesculapius, son of Apollo (often referred to as the god of medicine or healing), was a physician who became a demigod associated with the curing of disease. A statue of Aesculapius stands with those of Hippocrates and Hygeia on the building's facade.

One time President of the Royal College of Physicians, James Young Simpson was a pioneer of the medical use of anaesthesia. He lived at 52 Queen Street and his house was the scene of a great discovery in 1847, when Simpson and two colleagues experimented by inhaling chloroform. They were immediately rendered unconscious. Dr Simpson later described the event – '*Before sitting down to supper we all inhaled the fluid, and were all under the mahogany in a trice, to my wife's consternation and alarm*'.

Dr Simpson was one of Queen Victoria's surgeons and when she gave birth to her eighth child, Leopold, under the effects of chloroform, the drug became very much in vogue. A statue in Princes Street Gardens honours Simpson, and a plaque inside St Giles Cathedral reads '*Thank God for James Young Simpson's discovery of chloroform anaesthesia*'.

Location	Charlotte Square, EH2, northeast corner
Map grid	1A
Architect	Robert Adam
Built	1795
Style	Classical
Cryptic clue	Numero uno

Address

1–2 Charlotte Square, EH2

'*Not much ornamented but with an elegant simplicity*' is how Edinburgh's Lord Provost (council leader) described his preference for the design of Charlotte Square. This was to be a gracious finale to the first New Town and built without extravagant cost. Robert Adam was paid £200 for the architectural plans and although he did not live to see the square laid out, his simple designs were used as a model for subsequent New Town development. Adam composed the north side of Charlotte Square to resemble a palace front, crowned with sphinxes at both ends. Alexander Steven who executed the building of the square lived at No. 1. It was designed to interlock with No. 2 and is discreetly grand, with fine interiors. Notice how high the pavement around the Square is – this was to enable passengers to climb in and out of carriages with greater ease.

Celebrated New Town residents included Joseph Lister who pioneered the use of antiseptics (hence the brand name Listerine); Alexander Graham Bell, inventor of the telephone; author of *Peter Pan*, J M Barrie; and novelist Robert Louis Stevenson who based the title characters in *The Strange Case of Dr. Jekyll and Mr Hyde* on a real life villain, Deacon Brodie. During the day Brodie was a respectable

citizen and Edinburgh town councillor, but at night he revelled in drinking and gambling. When Brodie's debts led to bankruptcy, he took up burglary, but was caught, tried and executed by hanging in 1788.

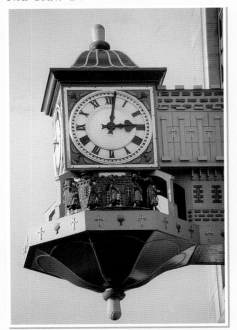

Location	Princes Street, EH2, north side of the street
Map grid	2A
Architect	John Ross McKay
Built	1935
Style	Classical Modern
Cryptic clue	What an Australian island has in common with a river in British Columbia and a North American fir tree

Address

Frasers, 145 Princes Street, EH2

As Frasers clock strikes the hour and half hour, a parade of tartan clad Scottish pipers travels around a circular track. Originally the pipers were accompanied by the tunes 'Scotland the Brave' and 'Caller Herrin' but now they march in silence.

Opposite Frasers is the five star Caledonian Hotel, built with such opulence in 1903 that its telegraph address was 'Luxury, Edinburgh'. It stood above the Caledonian Railway's Edinburgh station (now defunct). The right-hand side of the hotel's arched front entrance was originally for passengers to access the trains below.

Countless celebrities, royalty and politicians have stayed at the Caledonian Hotel but none are as singular as the four-legged

megastar who visited in 1954. Roy Rogers, the Hollywood cowboy, led Trigger the wonder horse up the hotel's grand staircase. Newspapers reported that the horse had slept in the Versailles Suite and they printed photographs of a specially laid bed of hay. Little did they know that Trigger had been smuggled from the hotel to spend the night at a local stable.

GLOSSARY
OF ARCHITECTURAL AND DECORATIVE TERMS

ART DECO (ALSO KNOWN AS MODERN)

A style popular in the 1920s and 1930s following an exhibition called the Exposition Internationale des Arts Décoratifs et Industriels Modernes in Paris 1925. Art deco was greatly influenced by the art and design of several cultures, including Egyptian, Aztec and Mayan. It is a streamlined look with clean unfussy lines and geometric ornamentation, for example, zigzags.

ARTS & CRAFTS

A movement of late 19th-century artists dedicated to retaining in the arts and architecture the hand-crafted skills of carving, stained glass, painting and sculpting.

BAROQUE

A style of architecture that was popular in a number of European countries in the 17th and 18th centuries. Baroque is characterised by flamboyant decoration such as statues, cherubs, caryatids, angels, scrolls and urns. In Britain, Baroque made a return in the late 19th and early 20th century.

BATTLEMENT

A defensive measure in which the parapet of a wall is cut out at intervals to allow missiles and arrows to be discharged from within.

BEAUX-ARTS

An approach to design associated with the École des Beaux-Arts in Paris in the late 19th and early 20th centuries. Buildings were usually colossal and highly ornamented. It was a favoured style for public buildings.

BRUTALISM

A style that flourished during the 1960s and 1970s, pioneered by architect Le Corbusier. The term originates from the French *beton brut*, meaning raw concrete. Buildings in this style are constructed with poured concrete in large unadorned block-like designs.

CAPITAL

The top part of a column.

CARYATID

A sculptured figure that serves as an ornamental support in place of a column.

CLASSICAL

A revival of Greek and Roman architecture and art. Buildings are symmetrical and restrained in adornment. Columns identify the style, used to frame doors, gateways and walkways. Sculptures and friezes are often a feature of classical architecture. Many classical buildings resemble Greek or Roman temples.

CLASSICAL MODERN

A combination of the classical features of symmetry and understatement executed in the Modern style with a streamlined appearance and geometric ornamentation.

CONTINENTAL AND ARTS & CRAFTS

A combination of styles that incorporate features common in Continental architecture with handcrafted decorative motifs. In the case of this book's photograph of 31 Castle Terrace, the central gable is Dutch styled and the protruding dormer windows look French. The decorated chimney block is an Arts & Crafts characteristic.

CORINTHIAN ORDER

An ornate classical column with a slender, fluted shaft and decorated capital.

CUPOLA

A dome that adorns a roof.

DORMER WINDOW

A window that is set vertically on a sloping roof. The dormer has its own roof, which may be flat, arched, or pointed.

DOULTON

A company established in 1815 by John Doulton and John Watts to produce porcelain and pottery objects. It went on to become Britain's leading manufacturer of industrial ceramics, tiles, tableware and ornamental pieces.

FRANCO-GERMAN (16th century)

In the case of the book's photograph of the Balmoral Hotel, this architectural description refers to the oversized tower and massive bulk of the hotel that is a German feature. The decorative details, for instance the dormer windows and ornate facade, are French.

FRENCH RENAISSANCE

Characteristics include mansard roofs, detailed facades, pilasters and giant columns.

FRIEZE

A decorative band, often sculpted, on the upper parts of a building.

GABLE

Triangular part of a wall at roof-level.

GEORGIAN

Georgian refers to the period in Britain between 1714–1830 when Kings George I, II, III and IV reigned. The favoured architectural style was influenced by Greek and Roman classicism and is characterised by understated, unadorned symmetry.

GOTHIC

Gothic was the architecture of medieval churches. It featured pointed arches, narrow walls, often supported by flying buttresses (the structures that supported the walls and roof) and buildings had a high, vertical appearance.

GOTHIC REVIVAL

The fashion for Gothic revival was popular in Europe in the 18th and 19th centuries, particularly for churches and public buildings. Sharp angles, decorative gables with no structural function, over-elaborate and pointed features are typical of Gothic revival. It is most closely associated with Victorian Britain.

GREEK REVIVAL

The revival of Greek classical architecture was popular in Europe and America in the late 18th century and early 19th century.

ITALIAN RENAISSANCE

Renaissance, from the Italian term r*inascimento,* meaning rebirth. It was a period of new thinking in arts and sciences from 1420–1600. The style of architecture looked back to Ancient Rome with round arches, arched stone ceilings, slender columns, domes and richly decorated facades.

JAPANNED

An object that has been japanned has been coated in a durable, glossy black lacquer. The style originated in the Orient.

MANSARD ROOF

A roof with two pitches (slopes). The lower slope is steeper than the upper one. Dormer windows are often set in the lower slope.

MINTON

Fine quality porcelain produced since 1798 and named after company founder, Thomas Minton.

MODERN

See Art Deco.

NEO-GEORGIAN

A revival of Georgian architecture.

PILASTER

Flat representation of a classical column in shallow relief.

SCOTTISH BARONIAL

Solid buildings with little decoration or refinement based on the fortified homes of Scottish nobility. Often with turrets, steep roofs and small windows.

SCOTTISH TENEMENT

A purpose-built block of flats.

VICTORIAN

The term Victorian refers to the reign of Queen Victoria, 1837–1901.

BIBLIOGRAPHY

John Gifford, Colin McWilliam, David Walker, *The Buildings of Scotland – Edinburgh*, Penguin Books (London), 1984

Allan Massie, *Edinburgh*, Sinclair Stevenson (London), 1994

FURTHER READING

Duncan Fraser, *Edinburgh in Olden Times*, Standard Press, Montrose, 1976.

Tom Hubbard and Glen Duncan, *Stevenson's Scotland*, Mercat Press (Edinburgh), 2003

Malcolm MacDonald, *Edinburgh*, David & Charles (Newton Abbot), 1995.

Robert Louis Stevenson, *Picturesque Notes on Edinburgh*, Broughton Books (Edinburgh), 1979.

James U Thomson, *Edinburgh Curiosities 2 – A Capital Cornucopia*, John Donald Publishers (Edinburgh), 1997.

Alan J Wilson, Des Brogan, Frances Hollinrake, *Hidden & Haunted Underground Edinburgh*, Mercat Tours of Edinburgh Publication (Edinburgh), 1999.